HISTORY'S BIGGEST DISASTERS

THE BIGGEST PLANE CRASHES

by Connie Colwell Miller

Blazers Books are published by Capstone Press,
1710 Roe Crest Drive, North Mankato, Minnesota 56003
www.mycapstone.com

Library of Congress Cataloging-in-Publication data
Library of Congress Cataloging-in-Publication data is available on the
Library of Congress website.
ISBN 978-1-5157-9987-0 (library binding)
ISBN 978-1-5157-9991-7 (paperback)
ISBN 978-1-5157-9996-2 (eBook PDF)

Editorial Credits
Mandy Robbins, editor; Bobbie Nuytten, designer; Morgan Walters,
media researcher; Tori Abraham, production specialist

Photo Credits
Alamy: PA Images, 25; ASSOCIATED PRESS, 11, 13, Ajit Kumar, 21;
Getty Images: Getty Images, 7, Manuel Litran, 19, Sankei Archive, 23,
Spencer Platt, 27; Newscom: ANDY CLARK/REUTERS, 17, GREG
BOS/REUTERS, 9; Shutterstock: Alexey Y. Petrov, 28, Crystal-K,
(people) design element throughout, MaxyM, (clouds) design element
throughout, Nieuwland Photography, 29, photocell, (brass plates) design
element throughout, sdecoret, Cover, 5; Wikimedia: Mztourist, 15

Table of Contents

Disasters in the Sky

Thousands of airplanes take off and land safely every day. But sometimes disaster strikes. The worst plane crashes in history are the ones that took the most lives.

Fact:

In 2016 about 3.5 billion people traveled on airplanes. Only 325 of them were killed in air accidents. That's fewer than one death for every 10 million passengers.

American Airlines Flight 587

American Airlines Flight 587 took off on November 12, 2001. It soon hit *turbulence*. The plane broke apart. It crashed in Queens, New York. This accident killed 260 people onboard and five on the ground.

260 total passengers

0 survivors

=25 people

*5 additional people on the ground were killed

turbulence–swirling winds that create strong air resistance; turbulence can quickly slow down an aircraft

When Flight 587 crashed it started a huge fire in Queens, New York.

Fact:

American Airlines Flight 587 crashed soon after the September 11, 2001 attacks. People worried it was another attack. However, investigators ruled it an accident.

The Lockerbie Bombing

In 1988 a *terrorist* set off a bomb on Pan Am Flight 103. The plane crashed into a field near Lockerbie, Scotland. The attack killed 270 people. Eleven of those people were on the ground.

259 total passengers

0 survivors

 =25 people

*11 additional people on the ground were killed

terrorist–a person who tries to create fear by killing innocent people or destroying property as a way to gain his or her political or religious goals

Emergency workers rushed to help survivors on Flight 103, but there were none.

American Airlines Flight 191

Just after takeoff, an engine on American Airlines Flight 191 fell off. The plane tipped and crashed. All 271 people onboard died. This 1979 crash also killed two people on the ground.

271 total passengers

0 survivors

 =25 people

2 additional people on the ground were killed

American Airlines Flight 191 crashed just outside O'Hare International Airport in Chicago.

Iran Air Flight 655

In 1988 the United States took part in a conflict in the Middle East. During one battle U.S. Naval forces mistook a passenger jet for a threat. They shot down Iran Air Flight 655. It cost 290 innocent people their lives.

290 total passengers

0 survivors

 =25 people

Mourners carried the coffins of the victims of Iran Air Flight 655.

Saudi Flight 163

On August 19, 1980, a fire started on Saudi Flight 163. The pilot made an ***emergency*** landing. But rescue workers couldn't reach them in time. All 301 people on the plane died from breathing in smoke.

301 total passengers
0 survivors
=25 people

emergency—a sudden and dangerous situation that must be handled quickly

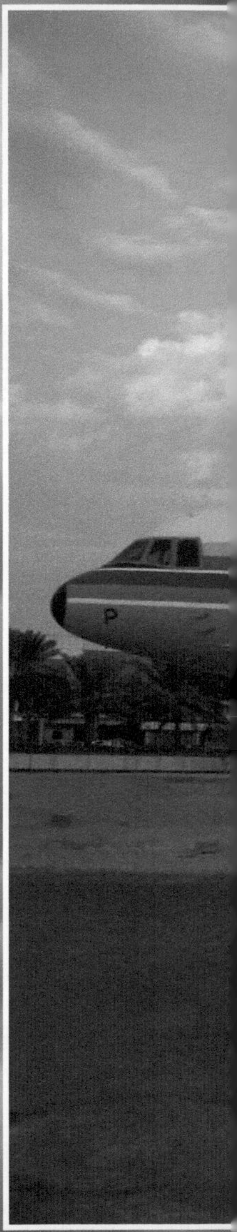

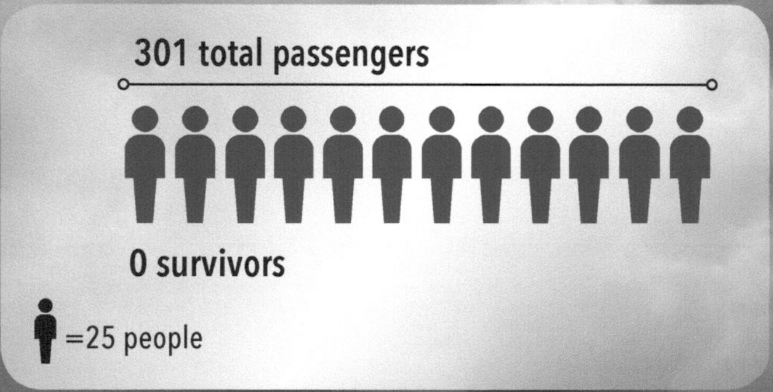

When rescue workers reached the passengers of Flight 163, they had all died.

Air India Flight 182

Air India Flight 182 took off from Montreal, Canada, on June 23, 1985. Terrorists had planted a bomb on the flight. The plane crashed into the Atlantic Ocean. All 329 people inside died.

329 total passengers

0 survivors

 =25 people

A police officer guarded the wreckage of Air India Flight 182.

Fact:

The bombing of Air India Flight 182 was Canada's most deadly terrorist attack.

The Ermenonville Air Disaster

On March 3, 1974, Turkish Airlines Flight 981 took off from Paris, France. Nine minutes later the rear *cargo* door blew off. The pilot lost control of the plane. Flight 981 crashed into the Ermenonville Forest. This disaster killed all 346 people on board.

346 total passengers

0 survivors

 =25 people

cargo–the goods carried by a vehicle; the area in a vehicle where objects are stored and carried is called the cargo bay

The crash of flight 981 slammed into the Ermenonville Forest, uprooting trees.

Fact:

After the crash of Flight 981, workers improved cargo doors and their latches.

The Charkhi Dadri Collision

A jumbo jet took off from India's New Delhi airport on November 12, 1996. Another plane was approaching the airport. The two planes collided. They crashed over the village of Charkhi Dadri. All 349 people on the planes died.

349 total passengers

0 survivors

👤 =25 people

Firefighters put out the fire caused by the Charkhi Dadri collision.

Fact:

The Charkhi Dadri crash is the deadliest midair collision in history.

Japan Airlines Flight 123

On August 12, 1985, Flight 123 was traveling from Tokyo to Osaka, Japan. The jet's equipment failed. The plane crashed into a mountain. The crash killed 520 people. Four people survived the deadly disaster.

524 total passengers

4 survivors

 =25 people

Fact:

Rescuers didn't reach the crash site for 14 hours. More people may have survived if rescuers had arrived sooner.

Flight 123 crashed into Osutaka Mountain.

The Tenerife Airport Disaster

In March 1977 a thick fog hung over the airport on the Spanish island of Tenerife. Two jets were about to take off. They crashed into each other on the *runway*. A total of 583 people died on board these planes.

583 total passengers

0 survivors

 =25 people

runway–a long, flat piece of ground where a jet can take off or land

Wreckage from both planes was scattered across the grounds around the airport.

September 11, 2001

On September 11, 2001, terrorists flew two planes into World Trade Center buildings One and Two in New York City. The buildings collapsed. Terrorists also crashed two other planes that day. Almost 3,000 people died in all.

nearly 3,000 total deaths in planes and on the ground

 = 25 people

Fact:

Some people do not consider the September 11 attacks among the deadliest plane crashes. Of the dead, only 265 were on planes.

A Safer Future

Plane crashes have cost thousands of lives. They have also taught people how to build and fly planes more safely. These improvements will help prevent future airplane crashes.

Glossary

cargo (KAHR-goh)—the goods carried by a ship, vehicle, or aircraft; the area in a vehicle where objects are stored and carried is called the cargo bay

emergency (i-MUHR-juhn-see)—a sudden and dangerous situation that must be handled quickly

runway (RUHN-way)—a long, flat piece of ground where a jet can take off or land

terrorist (TER-uhr-ist)—a person who tries to create fear by killing innocent people or destroying property as a way to gain his or her political or religious goals

turbulence (TUR-byoo-luns)—swirling winds that create strong air resistance; turbulence can quickly slow down an aircraft

Read More

Hammelef, Danielle S. *Building an Airplane.* See How It's Made. North Mankato, Minn.: Capstone Press, 2014.

Perish, Patrick. *Survive a Plane Crash.* Minneapolis: Bellwether Media, Inc., 2017.

Surges, Carol S. *The Science of a Plane Crash.* Disaster Science. Ann Arbor, Mich: Cherry Lake Publishing. 2014.

Internet Sites

Use FactHound to find Internet sites related to this book.

Visit *www.facthound.com*

Just type in 9781515799870 and go.

 Check out projects, games and lots more at **www.capstonekids.com**

Index